Presenting Sponsor

Supporting Sponsor

www.brookgreen.org

ENVIRONMENTAL IMPACT is produced by David J. Wagner, L.L.C.
David J. Wagner, Ph.D., Curator/Tour Director, davidjwagnerllc.com.

these photos sing. Like most of my work since the 1970s, these pictures illustrate the complicated tension between the sublime beauty and brash hubris common in most heavily altered landscapes. This double dose of aesthetic depth nourishes the germ of curiosity and reflection - essential elements in any conversation about the environment we all help create.

ASARCO El Paso Copper smelter in early stage of demolition (aerial), view from over Ciudad Juárez looking northwest, June 2011: Artists photographing from an airplane used to be uncommon. By now, most photographers who look seriously at landscapes have made aerial pictures. The view from 900 feet above the ground is one of the best ways to understand how topography dictates human activity. Rivers and mountains determine where we put railroads, cities, and industrial sites. Even this sprawling copper smelter complex has an organic relationship to the natural landscape – a realationship made clearer from this aerial vantage point.

Forty-two-inch gas pipeline section at construction staging area near Sinclair, Carbon County, Wyoming, 2006: This is one of a dozen pressurized gas pipelines buried in Wyoming's Interstate 80 corridor between Nebraska and Utah. The pipes range in diameter from 2" to 42", and in age from new to more than a half-century old. Scars over the pipeline trenches in the desert remain visible from the air for decades; destruction of native surface soils precludes recovery of natural flora over the pipeline for centuries.

Kent Ullberg, Corpus Christi, TX
Requiem: Contemporary artists reflect the concerns of their time. Considering that one of the most important issues today is our global concern about the environment, nothing could be more logical for a contemporary artist than nature's images. In my work I like to celebrate the infinite beauty I perceive in nature and hopefully communicate this feeling of preciousness to my public. But, this darker expression reflects my sadness at the violation perpetrated on the most pristine and beautiful parts of our country. An eagle is the obvious metaphor.

Interdependency: As an art student I became fascinated with the famous renaissance painting, "Vertumnus" by Archimboldo, a portrait of Emperor Rudolf II, created from all forms of vegetables and fruits. In this sculpture I use the same approach to simulate the interdependency of marine life in an ecosystem at the Texas coast. Forty-six different species from microscopic plankton to mammals, come together to create the sculpture of a tarpon (a specie itself dependent on several ecosystems). This is also a symbol for interdependency in all of nature, where we too play a part.

Bart Walter, Westminster, MD
Climate Change: Due to myriad causes, the earth's climate is always in a state of flux - why else would discussing weather be such a universal and favorite topic? Yet changes have accelerated and it seems human beings may well be responsible. There will be consequences; for us and for the other creatures we share this planet with. My sculpture, *Climate Change* is intended to initiate thought and create dialog. Is the ice in the sculpture melting or is it frozen hard? Is the Polar Bear questing for suitable habitat while stranded atop this ice, or is he simply testing the wind for scent of his favorite food (seals) from a convenient perch in his habitat? I have left it up to the viewer to decide how to interpret this sculpture and what the outcome may be for this bear. My hope is that the viewer will also consider how to interpret the flood of data coming in concerning climate change and what the outcome of the larger picture may be.

Suze Woolf, Seattle, WA
The Landscape of Fire: *The Landscape of Fire* is derived from a fire at Vermillion Pass, which straddles Kootenay National Park in BC and Banff National Park in Alberta. My immersion in the outdoors makes me acutely aware of threats to it. In the mountains, I've watched familiar glaciers recede and burned-over areas expand. The remains of forest fires are simultaneously disturbing and strangely beautiful. Unfamiliar tree forms are exposed. Hidden terrain features become visible. Greens, blues, browns are inverted. While forest fires are part of a natural cycle, global warming affects normal fire regimes, leading to complex second-order effects. Insect invasions, erosion, microclimate temperature extremes, and other impacts increase the volatility of change. British Columbia's vast diseased forests have become a net carbon source, where once they were a sink. In 2011, researchers hypothesized that fire cycles are now so frequent that forests in Yellowstone National Park will transform into grasslands. I began painting conventional landscapes of distressing subject matter, increasing in scale. I realized that the fire-scar patterns fascinate me. The biological structure of the tree interacts with the physics of the fire to produce an artifact that is both unique to that tree and similar to all others. My most recent burnscapes focus on individual trees. Because the works are watercolor on paper, I am not limited to a rectangle, so I score and tear the edges to match the contour of the tree. There are multiple ironies here: subject matter - beauty found in terrible things, and terrible things in all that beauty. And medium: watercolor has connotations of the well-off tourist, a kind of genteel "nice-ness" - I strive to demonstrate it as a medium of aesthetic and emotional impact.

sits on a stool in a human-like position with a trainer on its back. The elephant's front legs dangle and its eyes look down toward the camera, while the trainer proudly lifts one hand up in the air. On the bottom left of the frame, a spectator's hands clap after witnessing the act. One part of me enjoys photographing circus animals. But another part of me questions the existence of such a spectacle for human entertainment. My urge to photograph comes from this conflict. While I do not want my work to be didactic, I hope that this image will reveal the beauty and complexity I find at the circus.

Carol A. Santora, PSA, Kennebunk, ME

Last Killed: The last Bali Tiger (female), *Panthera tigris balica*, was killed on September 27, 1937. This is one of the only Balinese tigers ever photographed. The subspecies became extinct because of habitat loss and hunting. The Balinese tiger is one of three subspecies of tiger found in Indonesia, together with the Javan tiger, which is also extinct, and the critically endangered Sumatran tiger. It was the smallest of the eight tiger subspecies and inhabited the island of Bali. It was very similar in size to the leopard and only about half the size of the Amur (Siberian) tiger. Even the largest Balinese males did not exceed 100 kilograms (220 lbs). Today, the smallest living subspecies is the Sumatran. Balinese tigers had short, dense fur which was a deep orange and carried darker and fewer stripes than the other subspecies. Stripes were wide and tended to branch out; between them small black spots appeared. Light areas were a clear white and there were unusual bars on the head. She sounds like a beauty. Females weighed 143-176 lb. and males 198-221 lb. Females measured about 6 ½ feet, the male 7 ½ feet. Look into the eyes of this painting and see what we can no longer enjoy…

Losing Ground: The jaguar, *Panthera onca*, is listed as "Near Threatened" on the International Union for the Conservation of Nature (IUCN) Red List of Threatened Species. During the 1960s-1970s, as many as 18,000 jaguars were killed each year for their beautiful coats. In 1973, the pelt trade was brought to a near halt, however today, jaguars continue to be hunted due to conflict with humans who live in fear of them, or view them as a threat to their livelihoods. Deforestation rates are high in Latin America and fragmentation of forest habitat isolates jaguar populations so that they are more vulnerable to the predations of man. People compete with jaguars for prey, and jaguars are frequently shot on sight, despite protective legislation. Over-hunting prey by humans forces jaguars to prey on domestic animals and fuels the vicious cycle of human-wildlife conflict. Once found here in the United States, this cat was hunted to extinction here in the late 1940s. Today, it is found in Mexico, but swiftly declining, and in Central America, with the strongest populations being found in Brazil, The Pantanal, bordering Brazil, Bolivia and Paraguay, Chiapas State, Mexico, and the Yucatan Peninsula, Belize. While jaguars are faring considerably better than the other big cats, they [remain] on the IUCN Red List of Threatened Species.

Roaring Silenced: Of the eight subspecies of tiger, three are extinct – the Bali, Javan, and Caspian tigers. Three more subspecies are Critically Endangered - The Amur (Siberian), the South China and the Sumatran. The largest cat in the world, the Amur (Siberian), has only 331 left in the wild and their population is continuing to decline. The South China, the most Critically Endangered, is numbered at fewer than 37 tigers. The reality is that no South China tiger has been seen in the wild for the last 20 years. And the Sumatran has less than 400 remaining in the wild. The Indo-Chinese tiger with a total remaining around 136 is approaching the Critically Endangered status. The Bengal (Indian) tiger, the most common subspecies, with 1,200-1,500 left in the wild, is listed as Endangered. The global wild tiger population is less than 3,000 individuals, down from around 100,000 at the start of the 20th century. There are between 5,000-10,000 tigers in the U.S. in captivity and 90% of them are in miserable roadside zoos, backyard breeding facilities, circus wagons, and private homes. Today, sadly, there are more tigers in captivity then exist in the wild. There is a continuing decline all over their ranges due to poaching, persecution, and habitat loss and fragmentation. The tiger has been and still is widely hunted throughout its range for sport, for the fur trade, and for the traditional Asian medicine market. For the medicine trade – no part of the Tiger's body goes unused. Its value is over $70,000. The pre-historic ancestor to the big cat, the sabre-tooth tiger, has been extinct for 9,000 years and solely honored on cave walls. If the tiger's decline continues with the remaining subspecies obliterated by man, they will join the sabre-tooth only to be seen and honored on a cave wall as well.

Martin Stupich, Albuquerque, NM

Iron pipe merging with alkali lake bed, south of Baroil, Sweetwater County, Wyoming, 2006: This is a remnant of a 1920s-era soda mining operation run by the Pettigrew family until the early 1960s. This 4-inch iron pipe rusting and merging with the landscape will, in another century, appear as a trail of dark dust on the playa.

Rio Tinto Bingham open pit mine, near Salt Lake City, Utah; View to northwest corner of the pit, September, 2012 and ***Rio Tinto Bingham open pit mine, near Salt Lake City, Utah; Switchbacks on the north face of the pit, September, 2012***: These two photographs were made minutes apart with the tripod planted in one spot. A break in a heavy autumn cloud cover at the 8,000-foot rim of the canyon was the luck that transformed the landscape and makes

unseen,
unknown,
but there,
a dark presence
leaving their
careless footprint
on our Earth

Rick Pas, Lapeer, MI
Parking Lot Sparrows: This is one of my first works that explores the human interaction with nature. We often overlook nature as we go about our day.

Robin Over-pass: This is another painting that shows the human interaction with nature. Does the bird make it? I set the scene and let the viewer decide what happens. Some people interpret my work dark and threatening, while others think it is humorous.

Derek Robertson, Balmerino, Fife, Scotland
After Bandrum: The subject relates to the imbalance of man's relationship with the environment he lives in and manages, and the forces that drive environmental loss and mismanagement. It makes particular reference to the persecution of raptors (a very peculiar problem to the UK and especially here in Scotland) and the destructive exploitation of the seas and rivers. Both raptors and seabirds are "pinnacle species" in the ecosystem: at the top of the food pyramid they are easily observable indicators of the health of the environment as a whole and - as recognizable and charismatic creatures - they are a lightning conductor for public concern.

Boat Song of The Puffin: The painting touches upon degradation of the seas and the impact of the development of industrial, large-scale fishing; particularly here in the North Atlantic and the effect this has had on wildlife and communities. In the scattered islands of the West coast of Scotland the intimate scale of commerce and fishing among these scattered communities has a personal, almost charming, character. I have often traveled between small islands on little boats with the names "Puffin", "Shearwater" or "Kittiwake" - but the environmental impact of scaled-up exploitation of the seas is having global consequences on the most remote of communities.

Diana Sanchez, Bogota, Colombia (now Washington, DC)
Happy: Zoo is a series of photographs that explores animal habitats in zoological gardens. In *Happy* (from the *Zoo* series), the bars from the indoor hippo enclosure cast a shadow on the deteriorating painted background. Through these bars, Happy the hippo is seen eating hay. In this photograph, there are sections within sections. There is the section where Happy is standing, the section on the right that leads to another part of the indoor enclosure and also the door that leads to the outside enclosure. The tight frame of the photograph emphasizes the sectional space this hippo lives in and makes it more claustrophobic for the viewer. I was drawn to photograph Happy because his enclosure is a reflection of the 19th century zoos, when painted backgrounds were not meant to create an illusion of the animal habitats, but were meant to tell a story about the architecture and the people of the same region as the animal. I photograph at the zoo because I enjoy looking and learning about animals. At the same time, I struggle with the knowledge that these are human spaces made mostly for entertainment. I hope the viewer of my work sees both the beauty and complexity I find at the zoo, circus, museum or any other space where we use animals for human purposes.

Two Tigers about to Hunt: Museum is a series of photographs that explores the inanimate taxidermy in the dioramas of natural history museums. In *Two Tigers about to Hunt* (from the *Museum* series), the dramatic lighting, plus the juxtaposition of the tiger and cows, suggests there is something about to happen between these animals. A painted background depicts a tree forest and the bamboo foliage adds to the narrative of a "wild" setting. As viewers, we are asked to forget about the dead animal body that was transformed by taxidermy, and instead imagine that we encounter these animals as animate in their natural habitat. I photograph because it further amplifies the illusion of a "wild" setting, making the question of what is alive become more complex. In a still photograph, the imitative motion of the taxidermy appears as a frozen moment. I composed to leave out visitors, who would otherwise break the illusion of looking into another world. However, the artificiality of the dramatic lighting and of the painted background makes it impossible to hide the human presence. I hope *Two Tigers about to Hunt* reminds viewers of the animal life in taxidermy and also enables them to contemplate the human desire to encounter animals in exhilarating moments.

Untited #3: Circus: A Guilty Pleasure is a series of photographs that explores the spectacle of performing animals in circuses. In *Untitled #3*, the bright lights point to an animal performance that is taking place in a circus tent: An elephant things has put an even greater danger onto the lives of bees, their colonies, and hives. This "infinite" form represents the eternal life of bees and our need to protect and preserve these wonderful amazing creatures.

MO-BEE-US

A Mobius strip
An unending story to tell
Forever with bees
May all of us dwell

Resisting man's foolishness
Gmo-pollution-disease
Our request for life,
Mo' bees for us please

Still Not Listening: The year was 1989, and I was sculpting three shorebirds to reflect their mating rituals of springtime, when the Valdez Oil Spill occurred. With one bird feeding next to one doing his mating dance, the third bird emerged not on its nest, but with wing extended and suffering in the entanglement of crude oil. Caulking "gun" in hand, I spewed out upon this pristine world black vinyl caulking, strands hanging from wing and engulfing this living bird. 20 years passed and the Gulf Oil Spill happened. Still, we are not listening to the bird songs. Recall when coal miners deep within Mother Earth's womb would bring a live canary into the mine. If the bird stopped singing or grew faint, it was a signal that the air was too thin and it was time to go above ground; retreat or perish. They listened to the bird song! Are we as intelligent as a canary?

STILL NOT LISTENING

mating dance
spring ritual
plundered by
technologies intrusion

dance of the dead ensued
echoing 20 years
our cries are still not heard

listen to me
your canary
in the coal mine

listen to me
it's time to
let your light shine

The Ploy: A beautiful killdeer plover when intruded upon will leave her nest and feign a broken wing to lure the predator to come after her. Then, she sweeps into the air and circles back to her nest. Signs posted to keep humans from entering nesting sites are attempts to protect a delicate species. But we intrude, if not by walking and leaving footprints in the sand, then by our greedy exploitations and leaving large, heavy carbon footprints on Mother Earth. May we look to the wisdom of our Native American Ancestors who spoke of walking softly on the earth and leaving gentle footprints behind.

THE PLOY

feigning my
wing broken
to lure
intruders away
they come,
greedily,
stumbling foolishly,
or

global resources leads to irreversible damage to systems, like rainforests, that sustains all life on the planet? The sheer abundance of ecosystems staggers the imagination. *Diversity vs Destruction* compares what exists in one tiny corner of the earth, but begs the question: "Is the gain worth the cost?" Scientists now have satellites that watch from space and see what happens in Africa effects New York and Japan. The inherent interlocking of ecosystems remains unknown by powerless humanity. Most look at the diversity of nature for daily survival and [are] still awed by its immensity. But those with knowledge and privilege remain short-sighted and calculate only profitability. Immediate gain and unaccountability falsely allows us to believe there is so much to make from it now. Believing technology will solve what we do not yet understand and resources can be "managed". Microscopic elements of *Diversity* cannot be manufactured. If we indulge in *Destruction*, and believe it is all ours for the taking, we fail to understand what is crucial to our existence in the future.

Trouble in Paradise: Civilized societies are able to mobilize and take action in a crisis. What can wild animals and pristine ecosystems do to persuade humanity not to invade and devastate their existence? Research and efforts to understand our human impact on the planet tells us we live an interdependent world. The idyllic existence of these long-evolved environments that contain uniquely evolved life forms is directly threatened by the deliberate fires humans set on the horizons. We "nibble" at the edges of intact ecosystems and they get smaller and less able to sustain themselves because of our intrusion. Where can these species flee for future survival? These millions of members of life's astounding diversity can't ask for help. Their existence depends on those who plunder them. Humans are destroying a paradise that cannot be re-created.

Ron Kingswood, Sparta, ON, Canada
Takken In Het Bos: When I decided to paint this painting, which in Dutch translates to "branches in the wood", I wanted to illustrate a certain interval of succession that occurs after logging or perhaps a natural occurrence. There are many phases of succession that over a period alters the newly formed landscape. The period I have chosen to depict is when an area has been cleared of large timber, and sunlight is availed to expose the shaded forest floor. Early in this newly formed locale, after the briers have taken over, young and slender saplings start to emerge. After a few years, a dense grove of developing saplings takes hold. So begins the cycle of life that for thousands of years before whether, fire, natural circumstances, or even the domination of our ever-growing civilization, this tenacity of nature is constant, and never ending. This winter portrayal of this newly established sector, gave me a reason to merge my two loves, abstraction and nature. Outlining the precise and literal references in this painting is where the narrative ends, and the conceptual and imagination part ways. Fashioning allegories from truth is what motivates and defines great artists, whether sculptors, painters or writers.

The Clearcut: In this painting, I have chosen to represent a straight narrative, without allegorical references. This painting was one of the first I executed using the thread of environmental impact that wandered through my paintings for six years. The harsh reality of forest removal is so necessary for our existence as a human's species to have survived throughout the centuries. In it, I have shown some assurance that Nature has an awesome proficiency to restore itself, showing a small shoot of rebirth.

Lisa Lebofsky, Bronx, NY
Petzval Glacier (Antarctica): My artwork presents viewers with awareness and sympathy for the plight of landscapes facing extinction as a result of human impact. To convey these changing and ephemeral environments, I employ very thin layers of oil paint brushed onto sanded aluminum. The aluminum itself is left exposed to produce a unifying luminescence that can either permeate each painting, or, if viewed at precise angles, obliterate the image. This fluctuating luster produces a transient quality that both mimics the subtle movements of light as experienced in nature, and enhances the fragility of these endangered scenes. I find inspiration and collect source material by traveling extensively, often to remote parts of the world, in order to immerse myself in different environments and cultures. I paint onsite or take digital photos to cultivate a library of images for later studio work. I seek out areas around the globe that are particularly susceptible to the impacts of climate change, and meet with local residents and researchers to discuss how this land is impacted. To a great extent, these personal interactions inform what areas and what subject matter is ultimately painted. Recent regions visited include Antarctica, Newfoundland and Labrador, Greenland, and The Maldives.

Leo Osborne, Anacortes, WA
MO-BEE-US: The Mobius Strip is a form that I have sculpted for many years at various times. It is a shape that is unending, infinite. Starting at any point on the surface of the ring, if you run your finger around that surface, it will eventually come back to that spot of reference. The honey bee is in global trouble. We are at the mercy of the bee for natural pollination of trees and plants for food reproduction. Man's pollution and interference with the natural order of

confinements, limitations or bottom lines. We are the architects of the future. Let us consider that we are indivisible from both our natural environment and from each other for generations to come.
 (*stones with a line or stripe banded all the way around are considered wishing rocks).

Sayaka Ganz, Yokohama, Japan (now Ft. Wayne, IN)

The Travelers: I create animals and natural forms from reclaimed plastics. Japanese Shinto belief teaches that all objects and organisms have spirits. I was told in kindergarten that items discarded before their time weep at night inside the trash bin. I have a great passion for fitting shapes together and sympathy for discarded objects. My goal is for each object to transcend its origin by being integrated into a new form that releases them from the stagnant state into something alive and resilient. This process of reclamation and regeneration is liberating for me as an artist. My sculptures encourage the viewers to think about the conflicts and divisions that surround all of us within the context of a greater harmony. When they are observed up close, there are discernible divisions between objects and you perceive them as individual beings. When seeing my sculpture from a distance, however, one can focus on the overall direction and even the divisions add texture to the flow of energy.

Peter Goin, Reno, NV

Bravo 20, 1986/2013: [The first date is the original date of the 4x5 Polaroid negatives/the second date is the date of the printing of the triptych.] This triptych explores Bravo 20, a military bombing site, with Lone Rock, center. This site is one of the numerous bombing ranges used by the Fallon Range Training Complex which is located in the high desert of northern Nevada. Lone Rock is within Paiute territorial lands.

West 7th Street, Reno, 1990/2005: [The first date is the original date of the 4x5 negatives/the second date refers to the date the triptych was printed.] Reno, Nevada reflects and represents many of the contemporary issues dealing with water quality and quantity, development, sustainability, and all of the perennial concerns involving conflicts with farmers and ranchers, urban inhabitants, and Paiute (Indian) points of view. This view of Reno 7th Street appears as if it were a (metaphoric) fort in the early West.

Karen Hackenberg, Port Townsend, WA

Shades of Green; Amphorae ca. 2012: Shades of Green; Amphorae ca. 2012, an oil painting from my *Watershed* series, depicts a glowing "green" row of six discarded plastic and glass bottles posed on a driftwood board in evening winter light. Aligned as if they are on display in an antiquities museum, the bottles appear to have escaped intact from a glass exhibit case, and then surfed ashore on ocean waves from the future. This salty and surreal array of discarded "green" products has arrived complete with a trompe l'oeil museum tag lying snagged in seaweed and beach rock in the foreground of the painting. Illustrating the ubiquitous use of the word "green" as "ecological", as well as "green" as "color", the painting equates common soda bottles with priceless ancient Greek amphorae, and provokes questions about the impact and value of 21st century consumer culture on future generations.

Guy Harvey, Grand Cayman, BWI

Gulf Life: During my visit to Alabama and Mississippi for an event, I had a chance to talk with many people about the impact of the Gulf oil spill that happened in April 2010. While we've seen the obvious effects on birds and other wildlife, this spill has also affected deep water, open-ocean, coastal ecosystems and has shut down a vital U.S. fishery. I had launched the "Save Our Gulf" campaign thru my Foundation. The Guy Harvey Ocean Foundation funds scientific research and educational programs to encourage conservation and best management practices for sustainable marine environments. These two paintings depict those species that were affected greatly from the spill. The painting on the left depicts the offshore species, a Blue Marlin, Mahi Mahi (Dorado), Yellowfin Tuna, Wahoo, Blackfin Tuna and a Skipjack. I have also added an Oil Rig in the background. The painting on the right depicts a Brown Pelican, Seatrout, Green Turtle, Redfish, Pintail Duck, and Royal Tern. I would love for people to understand that we have a responsibility to care about and research the long-term residual effects the oil will have on sea life.   If we want to enjoy recreational fishing or have sea food to eat in the future, we have to be able to preserve the life that's out there.

Mary Helsaple, Sedona, AZ

Diversity vs Destruction [diptych]: Every day, modern human impact results in loss of native plants, animals, ecosystems and cultures before their true value is understood. Medicines derived from intact ecosystems take a back seat to politics and wars waged for resource domination. We make choices before we realize what will be irrevocably altered. The future of the diversity of life depends on sustainable choices, personal restraint, and global cooperation. The majority of civilization thinks we are at a tipping point. Will our generation be the first to recognize that exploitation of he loved – and Lisa Lebofsky – an accomplished painter who had already been traversing the globe creating artwork about the beauty and fragility of remote landscapes – to participate in this expedition. Scattering Rena's ashes in Greenland amidst the melting Arctic ice compelled the artists to address the concept of saying goodbye on scales both global and personal – to a human being and a landscape. Greenland's ice and permafrost will continue to melt as the planet adjusts to our carbon emissions. It is inevitable, and therefore crucial to render and honor these icescapes in flux, and help bring awareness to the many whose lives will be affected. To this end, Forman, Denny and Lebofsky conceived bodies of work in their respective mediums of large-scale pastel drawings, video, and oil painting on aluminum. In April 2013, the artists participated in a residency and exhibition at the New Bedford Whaling Museum, in conjunction with an exhibit on William Bradford, entitled *Arctic Visions: Away then Floats the Ice-Island.* Continuing the story of polar melt, which is a contributing factor to the rising seas, Forman, Denny, and Lebofsky followed the meltwater from the Arctic to the equator. They spent September 2013 in the Maldives, the lowest and flattest country in the world, collecting material and inspiration to create work celebrating and representing a nation that could be entirely underwater within this century. During their month on the islands, the artists shared the concept of their project with children on the islands, inviting them to document their homeland as it transforms throughout their lives. The children, using their creativity, can continue spreading awareness while inwardly processing the ecological transformations surrounding them. *Ice to Island* continues to evolve and take shape through drawings, paintings, film, performance, and education. Future exhibition plans involve a group showing of the three artists' work, as well as other artists' work pertaining to the subject of climate change, specifically ice melt and sea level rise. Media will include large-scale pastel drawings, oil paintings on aluminum, photography, ice sculpture, film, and multimedia installation.

Walter Ferguson, Beit Yanai, Israel
Save the Seashore - Man throws his flotsam and jetsam which pollutes the sea, and the sea throws it back at Man and pollutes the seashore leaving little room for simple recreation.

Save the Earth: This is a surrealistic, symbolic expression of the treatment of the environment by those people who have no regard for visual pollution and trash the world.

Apocalypse - As the air, land, and water are polluted, the egrets flying out of the picture symbolize the end when there is no where left to go.

Zaria Forman, Brooklyn, NY
Maldives #1: I spent September 2013 in the Maldives, the lowest and flattest country in the world, collecting material and inspiration to create a body of work celebrating and representing a nation that could be entirely underwater within this century. Exploring the tiny islands gave me a sense of both the power and the fragility of the landscape. The looming, vast ocean demanded my attention, as it tightly surrounded each island. The color, clarity, and warmth of the water endlessly invited me while the waves crashed ominously along the encroaching coastline. My biggest challenge with this series has been to depict the landscape honestly, conveying its utopian allure as well as the imminent threat that emanates from the rising ocean. These opposing sentiments are depicted in Maldives #1, communicating both the beauty and terror that I encountered. My drawings invite viewers to share the urgency of climate change in a hopeful and significant way. Art can facilitate a deeper understanding of any crisis, helping us find meaning and optimism in shifting landscapes.

Britt Freda, Burton, WA
Things That Sting: What happens if the things that sting no longer forage in our fields or buzz in our ears? This painting is set in an abstractly natural landscape, but without the complex diversity of different grasses, plants or flowers the uniform filed is potentially representative of a monoculture environment. The bees in this painting are dead. The presence of these visually alluring carcasses asks the viewer to contemplate what happens to our world if our human existence dramatically impacts the natural balance and order of a biodiverse ecosystem on which we are dependent.

When Building Cairns, Use Wishing Rocks, is thick with a layered, bright palate in an abstractly diverse, complex, rich, bountiful, raw, harvest landscape with five vibrant, gold bees collecting nectar and pollen. On the left stands a substantial cairn, indicating a marker along a path. Amidst the flora are more wishing rocks, possibly a result of a fallen cairn, certainly a reference to the potential to build anew. In the background stands a large/old deciduous tree referencing the inevitable passage of seasons from peak abundance to one of restorative dormancy. As we look forward in time we are reminded by natural cycles that the death component of winter births a tender verdant spring. The title of this painting asks the viewer to consider that when we build the path for the next generations we use deep desires of hopes and dreams, opposed to we have created; a monster by our own undoing. Yet, paradoxically and without forgiveness, we are also a combined force of a witness, a species clearly in tune with its own hemorrhaging powers and the sensibility and coherence of thought to know we are in trouble and something must be done to correct a mistaken course.

As we approach 9, 10 possibly 11 or 12 billion Homo sapiens, our reckless indifference to an ungainly foothold tells a story that Wagner has carefully laid out with 75 brilliant works of contemporary art and commentary on the current ecological crisis. This was not an easy task of fitting pastoral parts together; or combining the best of a certain theme—horses, women sowing, men in court, even smokestacks. Indeed, there has rarely if ever been such an exhibition wherein the madness of civilization has been so forcefully and elegantly told; such beauty and rich intelligence brought to bear on so much ill-boding imagery; and so colossal and enduring a menace as that represented by ourselves, in so beautiful a choreography.

It is as if beauty has been harnessed to foretell the end, not unlike those wondrous engines of doom pictured by Gustave Doré in his illustrations of Dante's *Inferno*, or of Don Quixote smacked silly by a windmill. We are on the ground, here; near death.

This exhibition—which could not have been easy to assemble—is a harrowing wake-up call and one that cannot, must not be ignored. If a "wildfire" in the Sacramento Delta, a landslide, freakish genetic engineering or the critically endangered Siberian Tiger, whose numbers are statistically approaching zero, are not enough to shake us from our complacent rut, then nothing will. Herein is the art of our age told unsparingly, without rhyme or metrical calm. It is jarring and depressing to the extreme, even as we inevitably marvel at the sheer beauty that humans can make out of misery; the glory inherent in our own destruction, and that of others who cohabit the precious Earth.

How is it we can pull this off, one must ponder? How can so much beauty be instinct within the decay and acid rain, gill nets and harpoons that herein are all too recognizable?

Eco-psychologists ponder the strange bedeviling that is our psyche and our out-of-control ego; the greed, callous indifference and outright cruelty of which we are, in part, capable. Capable translates into culpable, and *Environmental Impact* makes it clear and palpable that there are no happy zoos; that Jaguars are losing ground and smelters demolishing our children's hope of clean air to breathe. What then? What new art form is likely to arise that can

redeem us in the face of a generation that could, if left unchecked, be remembered not for art, or destruction for arts' sake, but for utter and unremitting desolation. Should that be the case, then this exhibition will be remembered as an all too fitting epitaph.

One comes away from this assemblage of fine art with a single hope: a flame of conscience that strangely, whimsically, soulfully wishes for something other than that which is before us. Let us take these measures of the human soul, these reflections on the passing of a generation, to heart: and resolve with all the incandescent and subtle threads that have been woven together in this exhibition so as to resurrect some other conclusion: the safety, tranquility, and assuredness of a future for our kind, and by our kind—for all of life on Earth. That is a new kind: a kindness of which we are made, as we are of drawing a bird, a tree, or regarding with hope and with awe and wonder the sunrise and the sunset.

If the history of landscape art has come to naught, then *Environmental Impact* is indeed a fitting tribute to a terrible end. But, as we would prefer to perceive it, this exhibition is a cautionary tale, done in finery and diversity, and just in time. It tells us with great intelligence, and splendor of what remains to be accomplished: not more stupid mischief and ecological unraveling, but the active remembrance of things past, and of the possibilities for a new tomorrow.

With an estimated 100 million species still sharing the planet with our kind (if one includes invertebrates and the myriads of bacterial and viral species invisible to the naked eye), there is every reason to be hopeful. To believe that we can succeed. The intelligence and prolific talent enshrined in *Environmental Impact* makes it abundantly clear that we have what it takes to survive, and to do so with nobility, virtue and generosity.

Picasso's *Guernica* reflected the horror of the Spanish Civil War, just as four-hundred years of Christian iconography mirrored all that was violent and religious in nature throughout the Renaissance. The countless Christs on the Cross, or the arrow-ridden Saint Sebastian were indicative of a dualism instinct in human nature. Yet, at the same time, those very impulses to depict tragedy were at the core of great art and sociological realism. If ecology is the global religion of the 21st century, then that same Christ-figure, as perceived by so many richly diverse artists, is the Earth herself.

Environmental Impact is no less indicative of seriously troubled times, and possibilities for the dawn.

Michael Charles Tobias, Ph.D. & Jane Gray Morrison President & Executive Vice President, Dancing Star Foundation 2013 © Dancing Star Foundation, dancingstarfoundation.org

1. http://www.earth-policy.org/plan_b_updates/2012/update102
2. http://www.forbes.com/sites/michaeltobias/2012/11/02/animal-rights-in-china/
3. http://www.forbes.com/sites/michaeltobias/2013/04/10/nigel-brown-a-new-zealand-original/

ENVIRONMENTAL IMPACT 2013 © David J. Wagner, L.L.C. davidjwagnerllc.com the conflict of the public's love of nature, and the sad truth of the democratization of Eden.

By the late 1940s, sensitivity to natural scenery had been clearly revolutionized: National Geographic's pictorial spread of the North Cascades' sublimity, after a similar depiction of Yellowstone many decades before by nineteenth-century painter, Thomas Moran, would result in runaway public fanfare and a storm of the earliest so-called eco-tourism and picture postcards by photographers most notably Edward Muybridge as to force the hand of Congress in their determination to protect over-crowded sites of world-heritage class stature. Whether over-crowding can be stopped in a world destined to add billions of more consumers hungry for wilderness remains one of the most troubling and unanswerable of conundrums for the artist and naturalist.

All of these conflicting attitudes and historic truths combine to inject countless ambiguities into the history of landscape art, and the environmental impact that has arisen in the historic and cumulative sensibility of protecting paradise, as it were. These are but a few among the many resonances of David Wagner's exhibition, *Environmental Impact*.

From New Mexico to Israel, Wagner has sought out works of art that lend credence to the all too-real truth of environmental despoliation occurring worldwide at this point in time. Ironies cascade, memories cry out to be forgotten, others recalled by way of vivid and disturbing testimony. In each work of art there is a quintessential nerve ending gone awry that beckons for remedy, re-attunement, some other emotion beyond mere sorrow and loss.

These artworks are populated by tragedy, or the symbol of such: Life receding into mute dumps, silent pits, poisoned cavernous wilds that deny wilderness in favor of human depravity. There are dead birds, desiccated horizons, ruined rivers, an escalation of toxic layers that mimic all that art better left to our nightmares. Yet, by nature of the assemblage and its theme, these artists and their creations have given us melancholy to think about and be moved by. Such is the chaos that enshrouds human contradiction, in setting after setting. This collaborative topography leaves no stone unturned in its ruthless laying bare of what it is, from quadrant to quadrant, neighborhood to neighborhood, that humankind is wreaking on the Earth in the name of occupation.

Fake hay, homes abandoned, lives lost. There are fumes, unchecked hideous developments, broken-down dreams, oil spills, death and despair: all this, in the name of human evolution beside the fantasies gone haywire of some perverse paradise that once was and, by all accounts, will never be again.

If this seems too harsh a commentary, the amalgamation of precisely articulated curatorial particulars makes it clear that this is no exaggerated desperation but the world of our own doing. If we are so desperate, why, then, do we continue to add insult to injury?

Write's Wagner, "Traditional art generally depicts nature in all of its glory, often in beautiful, pristine conditions. The 75 paintings, photographs, prints, installations, and sculptures in *Environmental Impact* are different than traditional works of art because they deal with numerous, ominous environmental issues ranging from the implications of resource development and industrial scale consumption, to major oil spills, the perils of nuclear energy, drought and diminishing water resources, global warming, and many other modern phenomena that impact people and the other inhabitants which populate the planet today."

From polar bears and dolphins to frogs, homes built on prime agricultural land, to the *Apocalypse* itself—this exhibition is unique. What do *Rising Tides* and Reno, Nevada have in common? Vancouver Island or a shrimp farm (formerly a mangrove) in Vietnam? These relationships are rendered sobering and unambiguous through the very humanity implicated in *Environmental Impact*. A pile of tires takes on the entire universe, as does a holding pond. The images in numerous media are, collectively, the heartbreaking truth—done beautifully, provocatively, barren, rich, resplendent, depressing, horrifying—all of the above and more. It is a terrifying prospect, taken together, of the human presence on earth.

In the juxtaposition of Walter Ferguson's little girl building sand castles beside a half-sunken tire in *Save the Sea Shore*, and Lucia deLeiris' intoxicating image of Antarctica's *Ross Sea*, are admixed the two most troubling of all intimations: a little girl's daydream, untroubled, perfect, intoxicating, and a distant nuance from the end of the world, as we now have come to recognize the signs—cracks in the ice, a melting continent, global warming, and the utter dismantling of a planet where life has evolved over the course of 4 billion+ years.

Antarctica's ice is nine miles deep, atop rock. But that is all changing, now. Not the rock, but the veritable pH of the Southern Antarctic Ocean convergence waters which, in turn, fuel the food chain essential for phytoplankton, krill and the entire marine mammal and seabird ecosystems of the Southern Hemisphere. The late explorer Thor Heyerdahl first detected DDT in the fatty tissues of penguins as early as 1968. Rachel Carson helped change all that, but so have the artists. From smokestacks to garbage dumps to birds with nowhere to migrate, *Environmental Impact* tells a story teeming with collaborative efforts by painters and scientists alike; a chronicle of woes at the beginning of the 21st century. These are not mere "inconvenient truths" but shattering realities.

Scott Greene's *Oasis*, a recent oil on canvas, in some ways says it all: dead lambs on a seeming altar that has taken the great Jan Van Eyck's Ghent Altarpiece (*Adoration of the Mystic Lamb* 1430–1432) and transmogrified it into the human story, a sacrificial lamb whose silent repose, in death, betrays all of the innocence lost; the beauty that belies the truth of our biospheric mortality. This is no accident, but the forensic evidence, sealed in artistic nuances of great insight, that in factory farms, with more pigs killed in China than anywhere else in the world.[2]

Art, however, has only ascended by its power to heal and to save, against the backdrop of such animal rights and environmental pain and impact. In the hands of great artists, art has been an agent of ecological consciousness raising and transformation. Classic examples include the seminal *Vision of St Eustace*, c.1440 by Antonio Pisano (Pisanello) in London's National Gallery; and Dutch Paulus Potter who, at the age of 22 painted *Punishment of the Hunter*, now in the Hermitage. Other remarkable examples include British photographer John Bulmer's 1963 image of a man and two dogs looking out over a grotesquely polluted city in *View Over The Potteries, Stoke on Trent*; disturbing photographs by Sebastião Salgado of famine in Africa, and oppression in Brazilian mines reminiscent of Charles Dickens' novel, *Bleak House*; and Nigel Brown whose disturbing, transformative work treats, among other things, the impact of British colonization—beginning with Captain Cook—on Brown's home country of New Zealand, as particularly figured in Brown's famed, magnificent stained glass project for the Auckland Cathedral (Parnell Street, 1998).[3]

Other environmental art clearly impacts in ways least traveled by, as in the case of one of the world's earliest signed sand gardens, that of the 15th century Ryoanji Zen Temple in Kyoto, a quiet scene of international solace and meditation in a city that had seen one of the most bloody civil wars on record—the Onin (1467-1477). Japanese connoisseurs of tea, flower arrangements and landscape art did not so much as fight back with their aesthetics as supersede the warfare with an attitude, an orientation to life that today most assuredly prevails in the Greenbelt of "ten thousand garden monasteries" that is the global divining rod of Kyoto.

There are no formulas for how the aesthetic conscience is likely to operate, let alone perform miracles. The outcomes of any seemingly ideological contests are a case-by-case experiment in human behavior and perception. Across the multitude of nearly 11,000 currently known bird species, their beauty in our eyes (and in their own eyes, as beholders of one another—as can scientifically be surmised)—has coincided with a mixed record, to be sure, of survival and extinctions, most usually at our hands.

The history of ornithological art—one of the greatest of natural history aesthetic traditions—originated in a frenzy of Latin-driven, science-based orientations, deriving from Aristotelian biology and culminating in such mammoth approaches to depicting the natural world as displayed by the great Buffon, Audubon, John Gould and J. G. Keulemans. It was this latter, prolific artist who supplied both Walter Lawry Buller (1838-1906) and Lord Walter Rothschild (1868-1937) magnificent paintings for their respective books on the *Birds of New Zealand* (1873) and *Extinct Birds* (1907) ushering in an era—in keeping with the transcendentalist calls for preservation by John Muir, President Abraham Lincoln, Ralph Waldo Emerson, Henry David Thoreau and President Theodore Roosevelt. Roosevelt took the art and activism of John Muir to heart, embracing Muir's unity of character, passion for writing, for fantastic metaphor, and re-invented America's future, knowing that the paintings of a Bierstadt, the chromolithographs of a Moran, and the photographs of a Watkins must translate into more than mere imagination: these were real places demanding real action, if future generations were to have an opportunity to see what the Earth truly was. Roosevelt, like the artists he admired—including photographer Edward Curtis, whose 20-volume *Indians of North America*, with its 2200 remarkable images—reimagined a future for all of us, at a time when Curtis, and George Catlin before him, recognized the signs of "a vanishing race" and, like Audubon with the Passenger Pigeon, realized that, indeed, people, cultures and civilizations could go extinct just like birds, should we fail to act in time to save them.

Sometimes the stakes were different than the protection of a big grove of trees in Mariposa, or a Yosemite Valley or Grand Canyon. Sometimes, it could be a pure and simple as a cow, painted by French artist Rosa Bonheur (1822-1899); or a coming storm as figured in so many works by the brilliant Scottish/American Luminist George Inness (1825-1894) who saw the juxtapositions of sublime nature and the onrush of modernity across the horizon. Such technically assured empathy as that displayed throughout much of the Hudson River School, for example, on behalf of multi-tiered sentience all around us would come to dominate the emerging environmental rallying cries of the 20th and 21st centuries.

E. O. Wilson's aforementioned study actually commences with an examination of the subject matter and probable motivations goading one of Gauguin's most salient, culminating meditations on human nature and the Tahitian landscape, his painting, *D'où Venons Nous/Que Sommes Nous/Où Allons Nous* (Where do we come from? What are we? Where are we going?).

It was Inness, borrowing from a precedent in Thomas Cole (the forest stumps in many of his paintings) who frequently placed a clear and active smokestack within an otherwise perfectly tranquil natural scene. This is most disturbingly clear in Inness' *The Lackawanna Valley* (c.1856) in The National Gallery in Washington, D.C.

By 1923, the very love and admiration of artists spawned overpopulation by tourists in the Yosemite valley, air pollution, the obfuscation of indigenous populations (the Southern Miwok, for example), and other blights, while a million automobiles entered Yosemite National Park to the tune of a park superintendent declaring that Americans should be able to visit this nation's legally enshrined ecosystems in this standard to which they were accustomed (namely, in automobiles). This mob of adulation accounted for the carving of an automobile-sized hole through a giant redwood, an iconic (even celebrated statement at the time) of

ENVIRONMENTAL **IMPACT**

THE GLOBAL AND HISTORIC CONTEXT FOR REFLECTING
UPON ECOLOGICAL DOOM AND RESURRECTION

By Michael Charles Tobias and Jane Gray Morrison/Dancing Star Foundation

Exhibition produced by David J. Wagner, L.L.C.

David Wagner's exhibition *Environmental Impact* represents a new level of broad yet focused appreciation for the sheer power, promise, and impact of art on the wisdom and sensibilities of current environmental crises. And crises they are. The myriad of artists, media and subject matter encompassed in the exhibition combine to convey a remarkable testimony to the urgency, persuasiveness and abundance of insights, perspectives, and power of art. *Environmental Impact* is packed not with empty mantras to a better state of being for the planet and all that dwell therein, or a blind and grasping homage to the beauty of life itself, but with deeply personal statements that range from lyrical epiphanies to thoroughgoing activist expressionism; from figurative paroxysm to surreal data-crunching.

Viewers of *Environmental Impact* will experience the beauty, the turmoil, the levels of ambiguity and mixed message, but may also feel unexpected pangs of hope, even pragmatic responses to environmental concern and outright disaster.

Take one clear example that serves as a fitting emblem for the exhibition: the lead painting, by famed Canadian artist Robert Bateman, entitled *Carmanah Contrast*. The Carmanah Walbran Provincial Park in British Columbia has been much celebrated for its huge Sitka Spruce, one of which is over a thousand years old and 314 feet high, amid a misty coast range of temperate rain-forest like luxuriance. This park was created as recently as 1990, following outpourings of protests by locals over clear-cutting that had been occurring in the area for years. Bateman's painting shows both sides of the story: The Creation, and human desecration.

In similar veins, Pieter Breugel showed, in his *Dark Day* and *Hunters in the Snow* (both painted in 1565) barren wintry trees populated by ravens, hunters and their dogs stalking game below, stormy peaks, frozen congeries of the human presence, suggesting a tenebrous looming angst symptomatic of our species' presence in all directions. But at least the trees remained standing. Breugel was likely unaware of the vast stretches of forests that had already been cleared throughout most of England, and Europe's lowlands, from Portugal to what is, today, Belarus.

Breugel, in his own manner, was an activist, focusing upon human despair and disruption on so many levels. Whereas his eldest son, the *Velvet Breugel* preferred to concentrate on magnificent renditions of paradise, Adam and Eve, of Noah's Ark and perfect flower arrangements. It was this latter nostalgic evocation of Arcadia's Golden Age that won over most artists of landscape throughout time.

That tradition goes back as far as documented art itself: to the earliest known records of Paleolithic aesthetic sensibility at places like Lascaux and La grotte Cauvet Pont d'Arc, discovered in 1994, with over 400 animal depictions; or the 5,000+ cave images recently found at 11 sites throughout northeastern Mexico near Ciudad Victoria; to Mesolithic images of animal life in regions where the rain curtain would subsequently shift, exposing stark yet revealing petroglyphs in desert canyons that joined with later Egyptian and Greco-Roman frescoes to suggest an incipient grasp of the power of nature over human consciousness.

This power—humanity's need and capacity, that is, to celebrate and revere nature—may well be the very key to humanity's survival, if not the biosolutions to the endowment and pertinacity of the rest of those species and populations that cohabit the planet with us.

We may, as E. O. Wilson in his 2012 book *The Social Conquest of Earth* intimated, have overwhelmed most other life forms (perhaps as a negative consequence of the enormous impact of our ancestor's transition to at least partial meat eating—hypocarnivorism—or one may so adduce) but our artistic reveries have only escalated in the wake of our seeming disassociation from the world of nature to which we were once so much more intimately attuned.

A 2012 Earth Policy Release by Janet Larsen, *Meat Consumption in China Now Double That in the United States*, shows how the Mandarin symbol in China for "home" is articulated as a pig under a roof.[1] Today, that pig is being slaughtered for human consumption tried to sleep at night. One of the lessons of Hurricane Katrina in New Orleans was that taking away coastal swamps and forests such as this one [removes one] of the primary protections from hurricanes.

Former Colorado River wetlands, Sonora, Mexico: The early 20th century environmental writer Aldo Leopold described his first visit to this region as a lush tropical paradise teaming with wildlife and plants. This is what the mouth of the long Colorado River looks like today. All of the water has been taken from it by the time it empties into the Gulf of Mexico. Some of the water goes to the cities of the American Southwest and California. Most of it goes to agriculture. One morning at sunrise, a local Yaqui Indian took us on a canoe trip through a marsh that he had created out of the agricultural wastewater. It was a small fraction of what used to be here but it was once again teeming with birds.

Irrigation, Imperial Valley area, Arizona: The economy of this region is heavily based on agriculture that is made possible by irrigation that is entirely from the Colorado River. Thousands of acres of prime farmland have transformed the desert into one of the most productive farming regions in California. However, south of the region the Colorado River no longer flows above ground at all for most of the year. My photograph of the mouth of the Colorado River in Mexico shows the result of this practice.

Polluted New River, Mexican/American border, Calexico California: This river flows from Mexico into the United States. The water carries much of the toxic waste from American companies that have set up shop on the Mexican side of the border. In addition to the industrial waste, the river consists mostly of agricultural runoff and municipal discharge. The river has been referred to as the most severely polluted river of its size within the United States. The entire flow of the river ends up emptying into the Salton Sea creating a very toxic mix fir people and wildlife there.

Lucia deLeiris, Watertown, MA

The Greenland Sea: I strive to paint not only the land and ice forms but a sense of the place itself: the expanse of the Greenland Sea: the way the sunlight highlights a contour of a glacier; the way it diffuses through mist and dissolves the edges of mountains; the way the polar light bounces off ice, blends into ice, emanates from within ice. I am inspired by sea ice: drifting, shifting, melting and refreezing, a drama of ice patterns I have watched in both polar regions. In the arctic landscape, I loved the endless intricate lace of sea ice revealed by patterns of turquoise melt pools, reflecting sky, clouds, sun. An occasional pool is patterned like an intricate jigsaw piece, revealing the hidden life below. There, seals burst up at a breathing hole in spray of brine. And there, a patient polar bear can feed her hungry pups. But behind the apparent serenity is a struggle for survival. With warming temperatures in recent years, the sea ice is retreating, and bears struggle to hunt. It makes me wonder at our own place on this small planet where human activities affect ecosystems as otherworldly as the Greenland Sea. I hope that my paintings will inspire new thoughts about the polar landscape.

The Ross Sea: During the ten weeks I spent living and painting in a wooden fish hut on the frozen Ross Sea in Antarctica, I reveled in the peaceful expanse of my surroundings. I noticed changes as the austral spring progressed from August through October and the sun rose slightly higher over the lifeless horizon. I began to hear ghostly pings of cracking sea ice. I watched a group of Emperors waddle in from the distant sea, rest nearby and continue inland. One night, through the wooden frame of my bunk I heard the strange wolf-like calls of weddell seals swimming underneath me through 6 feet ice. Soon, after the air had warmed to minus 20 degrees, I stepped out one morning to find the ice dotted with seals, as females were hauling up through widening cracks to give birth to scrawny pups. Depending on miles of sea ice to protect them from hungry orcas, the nursing pups grew quickly into their wrinkled furry skins. As I woke each day to find newly developed cracks with the progressing spring, part of the annual cycle of seasons, I realized just how fragile this icy environment is, and how sensitive it is to small temperature changes. As the Earth warms, I wonder how long this magical place will be a part of our world.

Drew Denny

Goodbye Ice, Goodbye Island, 2013, Continuous Loop Video on DVD (short form version: 10 minutes), Drew Denny, Writer, Director, Cinematographer, Producer: American artists Zaria Forman, Drew Denny, and Lisa Lebofsky traveled to Greenland and the Maldives together to document Earth's shifting landscape and the effects of progressive climate change. Their story invites viewers to share the urgency of the Greenlandic and Maldivian predicaments in a productive and hopeful way. The goal is to facilitate a deeper understanding of these crises, helping to find meaning and optimism amidst the chaos of melting, sinking ground. Forman led an expedition in Greenland titled *Chasing the Light* in August, 2012. It was the second expedition to the Northwest Coast whose mission was to create art inspired by the area's dramatic geography. The first was in 1869, led by the American painter William Bradford. Forman's mother, fine art photographer Rena Bass Forman, had conceived the idea for the voyage, but did not live to see it through. During the months of her illness, her dedication to the expedition never wavered, and Zaria promised to carry out her mother's final journey. Zaria reached out to Drew Denny – an award-winning filmmaker whose first feature film presented Denny's own journey to scatter her father's ashes across the American southwest in order to celebrate his memory in the landscape

Traditionally, the Indian tribes along the west coast depended upon fish for survival, but today, commercial fishing is so sophisticated that the Indians can't compete. Even if they could, industrial fishing methods have left their traditional fishing grounds depleted. On the lower right is a logging truck representing an approach to nature very different from that of the native North Americans. The logs on this monster are uniform in species and size, part of a plantation put in after an old-growth forest has been cleared out (from *Robert Bateman: An Artist in Nature*, pg.171-2).

Wildlife Images: In *Wildlife Images*, I have tried through my choice of subjects to depict the harm that man, by design or through carelessness, does to the environment. The upper panel shows a bald eagle whose wing has been injured by some gun-toting, yahoo hunter; it will never fly again. The middle panel shows a seal tangled in nylon driftnet. Thousands of miles of such plastic drift net are set in the Pacific every day, and miles of it are lost. These "ghost" nets keep fishing for years, catching everything in their path. This seal is doomed either to starve or strangle as it grows. In the centre of the panel at the bottom are two dead birds, a red-necked grebe and an immature rhinoceros auklet. The bodies of these two, along with many others, were found off the coast of British Columbia. What killed them is unknown, but the area where they were recovered was the scene of a major oil spill a few years ago. Almost certainly their deaths are related to the effect of oil on the maritime food chain. The images at the bottom left and bottom right, appropriately enough, show two of the many menaces faced by sea creatures - oil spills and a prime example of the junk filling our seas, a plastic six-pack holder (from *Robert Bateman: An Artist in Nature*, pg. 172).

Chapel, San Francisco, CA
Bound: *Bound* is a graphic exploration of the connectivity of all things. We and our environment are inextricably linked. Modern science has demonstrated beyond all doubt that an effect at the lowest level of life will find its way up the food chain to eventually impact us. The more we destroy, the more uninhabitable this planet will become. The original inhabitants of this continent understood this at an instinctive level and that is the reason I chose to flavor this sculpture with seasoning of Native American mythology. These ravens, which often represented the Trickster/Creator, are bound to dead trees in a denuded forest. Artists often use mirrors to study the reflection of their work; the mirror image often points up inaccuracies, imperfections, or fallacies, or outright mistakes in the work. In this case I used the mirror image of these bound ravens to show the bound skeletal remains of human bodies; the devastating consequence of ignoring the changing climate and environment around us. The ravens are cast bronze, mounted to a stainless steel mirror with sand blasted images. The stone on the side is marble.

Rising Tides: Sea Turtles and other aquatic life are now poised to inherit a huge new portion of our planet...If they can survive the increased pollution that is steadily warming our world. In the present a green sea turtle is ghosting through the ocean, in its element. On the other side the symbol of that turtle is cruising up the side of a flooded building. I have been diving with these animals in tropical seas for over thirty years. The amount of dead and dying coral has so dramatically increased at the reefs I return to year after year [and] is shocking. The rising sea levels in the South Pacific are already displacing residents of American Territories out there...Our future if we don't come to our senses soon. *Rising Tides* is cast bronze with a limestone cap, in an edition of twenty one.

Robert Dawson, San Francisco, CA
Homes built on prime farmland, Discovery Bay, CA: Discovery Bay is a planned, waterfront community. Many homes have private docks with access to the Sacramento-San Joaquin River Delta. It was built on land known as the Byron Tract, which was previously used for growing barley and potatoes. It was built upon the rich lands of the Delta that are some of the richest agricultural lands in the world.

Karahnjukar dam, Iceland: When I took this photograph the Karahnjukar dam was under construction in the Central Highlands of Iceland. It is the centerpiece of five dams being built there and was the largest dam built in Europe. The entire output of the electricity generated here goes to power an Alcoa aluminum smelter rather than Iceland's power grid. The aluminum produced here is now used to produce cans for soft drinks worldwide. The area around the dam is in the second largest (formerly) unspoiled wilderness in Europe. Approximately 70% of the workforce was composed of foreign workers which did not help alleviate the high unemployment of rural Iceland.

Former mangrove forest, now shrimp farm, Cam Rahn Bay Vietnam: In 1999, I traveled to Vietnam and Cambodia to explore the site of one of the most divisive wars of my lifetime. I went there with my brother-in-law John Manchester who had flown helicopters during the war and we visited the sites where he had been stationed. I had been a student during this time protesting against the war. The trip was an important way of dealing with this terrible conflict for both of us. After spending twenty years photographing water throughout the American West, I used this trip to explore water in the broader international context of Southeast Asia. Cam Rahn Bay had been an important American naval base during the war. The shore had once been lined with vast mangrove swamp forests. When we were there in 1999 the forests had been removed and shrimp farms were everywhere. The sound of the diesel generators stayed with us even as we

Environmental Impact!

Artists' Statements

Chester Arnold, Sonoma, CA

Holding Pond: How could anyone who has ever seen an open pit mine not be terrified and fascinated at the same time? The famous Meteorite crater in the southwest is the closest impact comparison. The curious ingenuity of our species to plot our own demise has been a theme of much of my work, and this is an early and prime example.

Miracle of the Frogs: this image of frog plagues in old testament narratives had something to do with this ironic reversal of a modern human plague on the world of frogs. Apart from the rich visual texture of amphibians as a source to paint, the ubiquitous asphalt covering we have created on the earth is another inescapable subtext.

Robert Bateman, Fulford Harbor, BC, Canada

Carmanah Contrasts: The aftermath of clear-cutting is an ecological horror story. The Carmanah Valley is one of the last areas of old-growth forest left on Vancouver Island and is home to a spectacular stand of Sitka spruce. But it is also threatened by big logging interests which have already clear-cut much of the surrounding rain forest. To help publicize this, the groups working to preserve the valley invited me and a number of other artists to go there are record our impressions of the forest. On our way to the valley we passed through areas that had already been cut down. Their appearance was shocking; nothing was left but stumps. In contrast to this scene of desolation is the lush, old-growth rain forest of the top panel. The human figure (me) is present to give some idea of the scale of the trees, but also to say that although humans do threaten these forests, there are many people working to preserve them (from *Robert Bateman: An Artist in Nature*, pg. 172).

Driftnet: During the 1980s, it was estimated that 31,000 miles of driftnets were set each night in the Pacific. These drifting "walls of death" captured untold numbers of dolphins, whales, pelagic birds (birds of the open ocean), sharks and turtles, along with the targeted species. Thanks to a recent United Nations moratorium on driftnet fishing, this highly destructive activity has been sharply curtailed in the Pacific, though it remains a common practice in the Mediterranean. But the underlying problem of wasteful over-fishing remains. In every sea and ocean of the world, the commercial fisheries are either at or over their sustainable limit. And the shocking proportion of what is caught is discarded. Conservative estimates put this "bycatch" at 20% of the total commercial catch. The plight of the world's fisheries is symbolic of a much wider and more vexing problem: the industrialization of what were for many thousands of years essentially sustainable activities of farming, forestry and fishing. Instead of treating nature with respect, we now treat it as a value-neutral commodity. Massive sums are borrowed and invested in large-scale technology, which must be constantly fed raw material in the form of crops, trees or fish in order to pay the interest on the original loans. When the "resource base" inevitably collapses, so do the economies that depend on it. It's a vicious cycle that ends in the devastation of ecosystems and the impoverishment of the planet (from *Robert Bateman, Natural Worlds*, pg. 36).

Vancouver Island Elegy: *Vancouver Island Elegy* is another cry of protest about the state of the environment, but it also focuses on my long-standing interest in different and time-honoured ways of life, particularly those that unfolded in harmony with nature. The top image displays an old totem pole of the kind found all along the Pacific coast. It resembles the coffin of a dying culture, a culture which, at its height, produced art to rival anything of Rembrandt's or Picasso's. In the middle, I have shown an Indian elder, a representative of the old way of life. I saw him on Vancouver Island at a gathering of natives and non-natives united in their opposition to clear-cut lumbering (the wholesale cutting down of forests when only the big old trees are wanted). The elder's face spoke powerfully to me of the vanishing of the old ways. This perception was heightened when one of the speakers, the tribal chief, told us the younger generation is not interested in their traditions - they are preoccupied watching sitcoms or rock videos on television. (I've made a reference to this by painting a TV aerial in the background.) In the bottom left-hand corner is an abandoned Indian fishing boat.

Artists' Statements

Brookgreen Gardens
Rainey Sculpture Pavilion
January 31-April 26, 2015